P9-DYP-468

September 11
Then and Now

PETER BENOIT

Children's Press®
An Imprint of Scholastic Inc.
New York Toronto London Auckland Sydney
Mexico City New Delhi Hong Kong
Danbury, Connecticut

Content Consultant
Christopher Gelpi, PhD
Professor of Political Science
Duke University
Charlotte, North Carolina

Library of Congress Cataloging-in-Publication Data

Benoit, Peter, 1955–
  September 11 Then and Now / Peter Benoit.
      p. cm.—(A true book)
Includes bibliographical references and index.
  ISBN-13: 978-0-531-25424-0 (lib. bdg.)   ISBN-13: 978-0-531-26565-9 (pbk.)
  ISBN-10: 0-531-25424-0 (lib. bdg.)   ISBN-10: 0-531-26565-x (pbk.)
  1. September 11 Terrorist Attacks, 2001—Juvenile literature. 2. Terrorism—United States—
Juvenile literature. I. Title. II. Series.
  HV6432.7.B427 2011
  973.931—dc22   2011007146

All rights reserved. Published in 2012 by Children's Press, an imprint of Scholastic Inc.
Printed in the United States of America 113
SCHOLASTIC, CHILDREN'S PRESS, A TRUE BOOK, and associated logos are trademarks and/or registered trademarks of Scholastic Inc.
1 2 3 4 5 6 7 8 9 10 R 21 20 19 18 17 16 15 14 13 12

Find the Truth!

Everything you are about to read is true *except* for one of the sentences on this page.

Which one is **TRUE**?

T or F Planning for the September 11 attacks began years before 2001.

T or F Only a few people escaped from the World Trade Center towers.

Find the answers in this book.

Contents

THE BIG TRUTH!

Hero Todd Beamer
was on Flight 93.

New York City firefighter at Ground Zero

The North Tower collapsed 1 hour, 42 minutes, and 5 seconds after the first jet crashed into the it.

The September 11 terrorist attacks horrified people all around the world.

6

CHAPTER 1

Out of the Blue

On September 11, 2001, at 8:46 a.m., a **hijacked** jet flew into the North Tower of the World Trade Center in New York City. A second jet slammed into the South Tower at 9:03 a.m. The hijackers' targets had been chosen carefully. The towers had been symbols of American wealth. Next would come an attack against a symbol of the American government.

 An average of 50,000 people worked in the World Trade Center each day.

In Washington, D.C.

Another hijacked jet roared low outside of Washington, D.C., as the world focused on the disaster in New York. The **terrorist** flying the plane had suddenly changed course over southern Ohio. At 9:37 a.m., the jet hit the west side of the **Pentagon**. A fireball rose where the plane hit the building.

About 24,000 people work in the Pentagon on a normal day.

The American Airlines jet did extensive damage to one section of the Pentagon.

A smoking crater in a field near Shanksville, Pennsylvania, marked the site of the fourth plane crash.

The Fourth Plane

At 9:59 a.m., the South Tower of the World Trade Center began to collapse in clouds of smoke. The North Tower caved in twenty-nine minutes later. At 10:03 a.m., a fourth team of hijackers crashed a plane in a field near Shanksville, Pennsylvania. Most people believe this plane was meant to hit either the U.S. Capitol or the White House. The four hijacked planes had resulted in the worst terrorist attack in U.S. history.

The 1993 World Trade Center terror attack caused massive damage to the underground parking garages.

CHAPTER 2

Planning Terror

September 11 was not the first time that the World Trade Center had been attacked. In 1993, a group led by terrorist Ramzi Yousef hid a bomb in an underground garage at the World Trade Center. Yousef planned to knock the North Tower into the South Tower and kill all the people inside. Yousef was angry that the United States favored Israel over most Arab nations. The bomb killed six people but failed to destroy the towers.

← More than 1,000 people were injured in the 1993 World Trade Center bombing.

The Base

Yousef had traveled to New York from Afghanistan. He had learned how to make bombs from the anti-American terrorist group **al-Qaeda** (al-KYE-dah). In New York, Yousef got money from his uncle, Khalid Sheikh Mohammed (KAH-leed SHAYK mah-HAH-med). Mohammed later confessed that he was a member of al-Qaeda. In 1998, he began to plan the September 11 attacks with al-Qaeda leader Osama bin Laden.

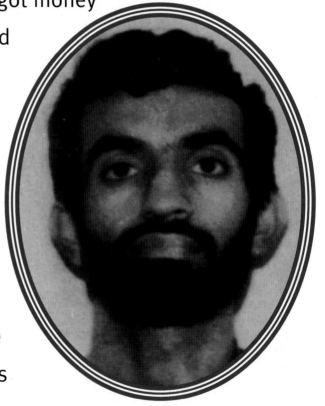

Ramzi Yousef was sentenced to life in prison plus 240 years for his crimes.

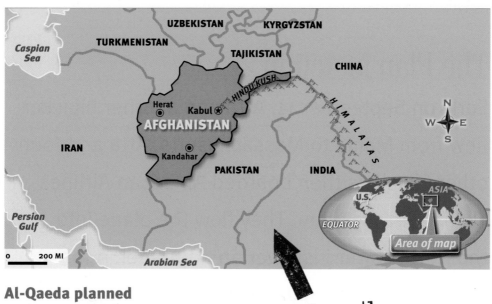

Al-Qaeda planned their attacks from hiding places in rugged and mountainous Afghanistan.

Al-Qaeda is the Arabic word for "the base of a structure."

Masterminds

Bin Laden lived in Afghanistan. The Afghan government allowed al-Qaeda to operate there. Bin Laden and Khalid Sheikh Mohammed chose al-Qaeda members to learn to fly airplanes. They selected Mohamed Atta as the leader. Atta moved to the United States. He enrolled in pilot training school and earned a pilot's license.

The Plan in Action

Early on September 11, Atta and another hijacker flew from Maine to Massachusetts. Atta and four other hijackers then boarded American Airlines Flight 11 at 7:35 a.m. They flew the plane into the North Tower just over an hour later. A mix-up prevented Atta's luggage containing plans for the attack from being loaded onto the plane. Investigators found it and learned the names of the other 18 terrorists. It was too late by then to do anything.

After September 11, the Federal Bureau of Investigation (FBI) assigned almost 7,000 agents to investigate the attacks.

Atta's life and actions were investigated closely after the September 11 attacks.

Osama bin Laden

Osama bin Laden was born in 1957 in Saudi Arabia to a wealthy family. After college, he went to Afghanistan to fight the invading Soviet army. His efforts received support from the United States. Bin Laden believed in an extreme version of **Islam**. He rejected many modern ideas and banned things he felt were un-Islamic. In 1988, bin Laden helped form al-Qaeda to fight what he considered the "enemies of Islam." These enemies included the United States and other Western nations. After the September 11 attacks, Osama bin Laden was the most wanted criminal in the world. He successfully avoided capture for nearly 10 years, but was finally killed in a U.S. military operation on May 2, 2011.

The collapsing towers covered the surrounding area with huge, dense clouds of dust and ash.

CHAPTER 3

Dealing With Disaster

New York City firefighters quickly responded to the attack on the North Tower. The fire department set up a command post in the building's lobby minutes after the first crash. Firefighters entered the tower to save the thousands of people trapped inside. Police, doctors, nurses, and other emergency workers also hurried to help.

The World Trade Center's North Tower was 110 stories high before its collapse.

The Upper Floors

People below the floors hit by the planes used stairwells to escape. Those above were trapped. These people fled toward the roof in hope that helicopters might rescue them. But the roof doors were locked. Smoke and heat made it impossible for helicopters to get close. A single open stairway allowed a few people to escape the upper floors of the South Tower. No one else on the upper floors of either building survived.

The attacks caused both towers to collapse nearly completely.

The September 11 attacks damaged four New York City subway lines.

Fire chiefs did their best to keep track of the rescue teams and manage them effectively.

Problems

Problems and confusion delayed rescue efforts. Dust and smoke were everywhere. The planes had damaged the towers' communication systems when they crashed into the buildings. Many firefighters had arrived so quickly that the fire chiefs on the ground couldn't keep track of them. The location of New York City's emergency management headquarters also added to the confusion. It was in a building next to the towers.

Underground fires burned for 69 days after the attack on the Twin Towers.

In a single morning, the collapse of the North and South Towers transformed the skyline of Manhattan.

Tragedy for Rescue Workers

Officials realized the rescuers were in great danger. They were able to reach officers in the North Tower. They ordered the rescuers to **evacuate** the building. Some rescuers were still trapped inside when the building collapsed. The collapse of both towers killed 343 firefighters and 60 police officers. It was the deadliest day in history for New York City firefighters and police officers.

Fleeing by Water

Debris clogged the streets. Subways and commuter trains were shut down. Tens of thousands of people had no way to get off of the island of Manhattan. A Coast Guard patrol ship put out a call soon after the attacks. More than 100 ferries, tourist boats, and tugboats rushed to the tip of Manhattan to help.

Thousands of people scrambled to leave lower Manhattan to get away from the falling debris and choking dust.

Civilian boat owners and operators, with direction provided by the U.S. Coast Guard, moved hundreds of thousands of New Yorkers to safety after the attacks.

Ordinary People

The Coast Guard worked with **civilians** to help make sure people were transported quickly and safely away from Manhattan. Boats helped at least 300,000 people flee the disaster area. They also carried more than 2,000 injured people to safety. Some boats also brought supplies and fresh water to the emergency workers.

Stories of Survival

Engineer Pasquale Buzzelli had reached the stairs on the 22nd floor when the North Tower fell. He woke up two hours later on a piece of concrete. He had only fractured his ankle. Another group of people were swept off their feet as strong winds blew down the stairway they were on. Somehow, they lived.

Rescue workers as well as bystanders got survivors to safety as quickly as possible.

Sixteen people survived the North Tower collapse.

The outdoor Pentagon Memorial, opened in 2008, includes 184 benches with one victim's name on each.

Attack at the Pentagon

American Airlines Flight 77 left Dulles Airport in Washington, D.C., at 8:20 a.m. Five terrorists armed with knives and box cutters took control of the plane a little more than a half hour later. The hijackers turned the plane around. Air traffic controllers soon noticed it heading for Washington, D.C. Flight 77 slammed into the Pentagon. The crash killed all 59 people on the plane and 125 others in the building.

Rescue Efforts

Military and civilian workers from the Pentagon braved flames and falling rubble to rescue survivors. The part of the building hit by the plane collapsed at 10:10 a.m. Firefighters couldn't control the flames until the next day. They put out small fires for several days afterward.

Extinguishing the many fires within the Pentagon took firefighters days.

"Let's Roll"

A group of hijackers took over United Airlines Flight 93 around 9:30 a.m. The plane had taken off from Newark International Airport about 45 minutes earlier. Hijacker Ziad Jarrah (ZY-ed jur-RAH) was now piloting the plane. He steered it toward Washington, D.C. Officials believe he meant to fly the jet into the White House or the U.S. Capitol. A group of passengers and flight crew members fought to retake control. Their actions prevented the plane from hitting its intended target and saved many lives.

"Let's Roll"

Todd Beamer was talking to a phone operator when the passengers made their move. At 9:55 a.m., the operator heard Beamer say, "Are you guys ready? Okay. Let's roll."

Desperate Moments

The passengers rushed the cockpit and began pushing their way in. Jarrah swept the plane from side to side to knock them off their feet.

The Crash

No one knows if the passengers got into the cockpit. Jarrah rolled the jet onto its back and crashed it, killing all 44 people on board.

People on the ground run to avoid smoke and debris as a tower collapses.

28

CHAPTER 4

National Tragedy

Americans reacted to the attacks with shock and horror. Nearly 3,000 people had died. People in other cities wondered if more hijacked planes might be headed for them. Military planes were ordered to shoot down any hijacked jets. The entire country was on alert.

The area destroyed by the collapse of the World Trade Center towers is called Ground Zero.

Taking Action

People soon began to evacuate the United Nations buildings in New York City and Chicago's Sears Tower. Officials worried that these buildings might be terrorist targets. At 9:45 a.m., the U.S. government ordered all planes to land immediately at the nearest airport. Planes flying to the United States from other countries were ordered to turn back or fly to Canada or Mexico. By about 12:15 p.m., not a single civilian plane was in the air above the United States.

Not knowing if more attacks were still to come, authorities evacuated buildings around the country.

President Bush's address spoke of reactions of "disbelief, terrible sadness and a quiet, unyielding anger."

President George Bush first addressed the nation from Barksdale Air Force Base in Louisiana hours after the attacks.

Leading the Country

U.S. president George Bush was at a Florida elementary school when he learned about the attack. He returned to the White House that evening and addressed the nation at 8:30 p.m. Bush's leadership after the attacks drew praise from the entire country. He soon announced a plan to track down the terrorists behind the attacks.

Many Arab Americans were treated poorly after the September 11 attacks.

Reactions Around the World

Countries around the world expressed their support for the United States and spoke out against the attacks. The United States and other nations began arresting suspected terrorists to prevent other attacks. This sometimes resulted in discrimination against Muslims and Middle Eastern people. Many innocent people were accused of being or supporting terrorists.

The Country Joins Together

Rescue workers from across the country traveled to New York City to help. President Bush visited them on September 14. He told the workers that the entire world was behind them. People across the country put aside their differences and united in support of the rescue workers. The attacks had ended up bringing the country's people closer together.

Three days after the attacks, President George Bush stood atop the rubble to address the rescue workers.

People from more than 90 countries died in the attacks.

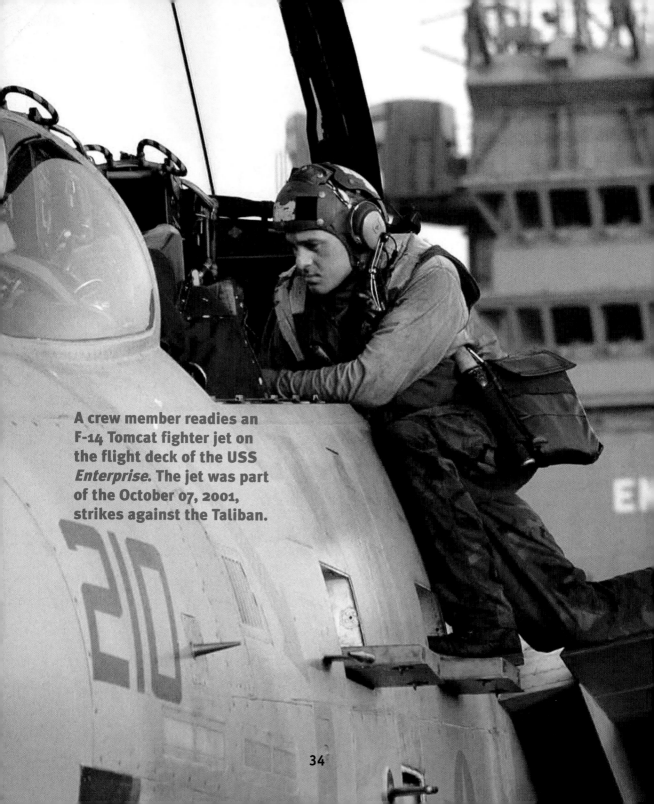

A crew member readies an F-14 Tomcat fighter jet on the flight deck of the USS *Enterprise*. The jet was part of the October 07, 2001, strikes against the Taliban.

CHAPTER 5

After 9/11

The U.S. government suspected Osama bin Laden and al-Qaeda of planning the attacks from Afghanistan. Officials ordered the **Taliban** to turn over bin Laden and the other al-Qaeda leaders. It refused. U.S. aircraft carriers soon headed for the **Middle East**. On October 7, the United States and Britain launched an attack called Operation Enduring Freedom. They wanted to remove the Taliban government and drive al-Qaeda out of Afghanistan.

Defeat for the Taliban

The United States, Great Britain, and others removed the Taliban from power in Afghanistan in a matter of weeks. The last Taliban fighters and al-Qaeda troops fled into the mountains along Afghanistan's border with Pakistan. Bin Laden and other al-Qaeda leaders escaped. Efforts to keep the Taliban out of power continue even today.

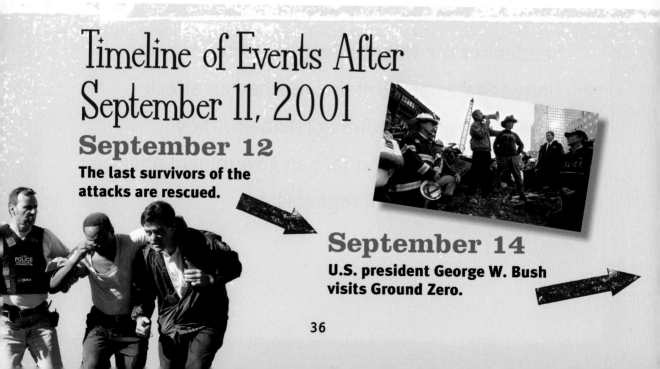

Timeline of Events After September 11, 2001

September 12

The last survivors of the attacks are rescued.

September 14

U.S. president George W. Bush visits Ground Zero.

Paying Tribute

September 11 became a day to remember those who had lost their lives. Memorials were built in New York City, Washington, and elsewhere. Classrooms across the country sent cards and letters to the rescue workers. People now visit New York City from all around the world to see Ground Zero and pay tribute to those who died.

September 20

The Department of Homeland Security is created.

October 7

U.S. and British forces attack Afghanistan.

The Concert for New York was organized by musician Paul McCartney and attended by many of the 9/11 rescue workers.

Helping Out

People around the country did everything they could to help out. They donated blood and money toward relief efforts. Music and film stars banded together for a concert honoring the victims. Even today, many communities host annual 9/11 blood drives. Stars continue to honor 9/11 victims with charity performances. On September 11, 2009, rapper Jay-Z held a concert to benefit the families of firefighters and police officers who died during the attack.

Remembering the Tragedy

Each of the locations attacked on September 11, 2001 has its own memorial. The Pentagon Memorial in Arlington, Virginia, opened on September 11, 2008. Exactly three years later, the National September 11 Memorial was dedicated at the World Trade Center site. The U.S. National Park Service is building a Flight 93 National Memorial on the crash site in Shanksville, Pennsylvania. It will include a 93-foot-tall tower containing large wind chimes.

Artistic rendering of the National September 11 Memorial in New York

President George W. Bush chose Pennsylvania governor Tom Ridge to lead the Department of Homeland Security.

Homeland Security

President Bush established the Department of Homeland Security (DHS) in response to the 9/11 attacks. Today, the DHS protects the United States against terrorism, natural disasters, and other threats. The DHS has seven agencies. One of these is the Transportation Security Administration. The TSA has tightened airport security to prevent terrorist attacks.

Helping to Heal

Many people affected by the September 11 attacks faced tough challenges. More than 3,000 children lost a parent in the attacks. Thousands of people went through counseling to help deal with anger, fear, sadness, and loss. Many rescue workers were sickened by the harmful **fumes** and dust. On December 22, 2010, the U.S. Congress funded a program to provide health care and money to firefighters, police officers, and other rescuers who were on the scene on that grim day on 2001.

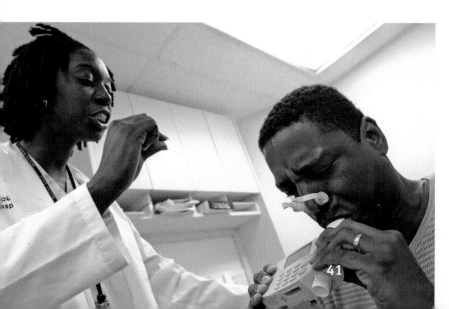

Federal funding is now available to help those rescuers and workers whose health was affected by toxic dust and chemicals at Ground Zero.

Closure at Last

In 2011, Osama bin Laden was discovered to be hiding in a compound in Pakistan. On May 2, a team of U.S. Navy SEALs attacked the compound. President Obama announced shortly afterward that bin Laden had been killed. Bin Laden's death helped bring closure to the millions of Americans who were affected by the 9/11 attacks. ★

When bin Laden's death was announced, people gathered at Ground Zero to remember his victims.

True Statistics

Number of September 11 hijackers: 19

Number of hijacked planes: 4

Time it took South Tower to collapse after being hit: 55 minutes, 58 seconds

Number of non-hijackers killed on September 11: 2,977

Number of firefighters killed in New York City: 343

Number of people killed in the crash near Shanksville, Pennsylvania: 44

Number of people killed in the Pentagon attack: 184

Number of people who survived the North Tower collapse: 16

Number of people evacuated by boat from Manhattan: At least 300,000

Did you find the truth?

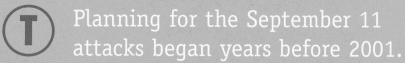

T Planning for the September 11 attacks began years before 2001.

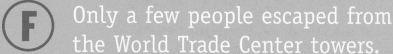

F Only a few people escaped from the World Trade Center towers.

Resources

Books

Anderson, Dale. *The Terrorist Attacks of September 11, 2001*. Milwaukee: Gareth Stevens: 2003.

Benoit, Peter. *September 11, 2001: We Will Never Forget*. New York: Children's Press, 2012.

Buell, Tonya. *The Crash of United Flight 93 on September 11, 2001*. New York: Rosen, 2003.

Englar, Mary. *September 11*. Mankato, MN: Compass Point, 2007.

Fradin, Dennis B. *September 11, 2001*. New York: Benchmark, 2009.

Ganci, Chris. *Chief: The Life of Peter J. Ganci, a New York City Firefighter*. New York: Orchard, 2003.

Gard, Carolyn. *The Attack on the Pentagon on September 11, 2001*. New York: Rosen, 2003.

Margulies, Phillip. *Al Qaeda: Osama bin Laden's Army of Terrorists*. New York: Rosen, 2003.

Organizations and Web Sites

History.com: 9/11 Attacks

www.history.com/topics/9-11-attacks

Explore a collection of videos taken on September 11 and read articles about the attacks.

9/11 Memorial and Museum

www.national911memorial.org

Learn about the national memorial and museum located on the World Trade Center site in New York City.

Places to Visit

Flight 93 National Memorial

1060 Lambertsville Road
Stoystown, PA 15563
www.nps.gov/flni/index.htm
View the place where Flight 93 went down in southern Pennsylvania.

Pentagon Memorial

1 Rotary Road
Arlington, VA 22202
www.whs.mil/memorial
See the nation's first major September 11 memorial built near the crash site on the west side of the Pentagon.

Important Words

al-Qaeda (al-KYE-dah)—the terrorist group responsible for the September 11 attacks; the name means "the base" in Arabic

civilians (si-VIL-yuhns)—people who are not members of a police or fire department or the armed forces

evacuate (i-VAK-yoo-ate)—to get away from a dangerous area

fumes (FYOOMS)—smelly or dangerous smoke or gas

hijacked (HYE-jakd)—stolen or taken over

Islam (ISS-luhm)— a religion based on the teachings of Muhammad; followers of Islam are called Muslims

Middle East (MID-uhl EEST)—an area of the world that includes Libya, Egypt, Iran, Iraq, Israel, Saudi Arabia, Syria, Turkey, and other countries

Pentagon (PEN-tuh-gahn) – the headquarters of the U.S. Department of Defense; its name comes from the building's five-sided, or pentagonal, shape

Taliban (TAL-eh-bon)—the extremist Islamic group that ruled much of Afghanistan from 1995 to the end of 2001

terrorist (TER-ur-ist)—a person who plans and uses violence to force others into obeying

Index

Page numbers in **bold** indicate illustrations

About the Author

Peter Benoit is educated as a mathematician but has many other interests. He has taught and tutored high school and college students for many years, mostly in math and science. He also runs summer workshops for writers and students of literature. Mr. Benoit has written more than 2,000 poems. His life has been one committed to learning. He lives in Greenwich, New York.